A WORLD BEYOND THE STARS

ELI HERNANDEZ

Printed in the United States of America

ISBN: 9798549571617

10 9 8 7 6 5 4 3 2 1

EMPIRE PUBLISHING
www.empirebookpublishing.com

ADVANCE PRAISE

If you were privileged to personally know and minister with evangelist Eli Hernandez as I was, then you would know him to be a man that spent a lifetime in prayer and in the study of God's Word. His was a ministry of anointed preaching, practical exhortation, and miraculous demonstration of God's gifts to men. He always left me desiring more—more insight, more training, or more explanation of how God was manifesting the outpouring of His Spirit during this present great, spiritual awakening. And, fortunately for all of us, he left some of his invaluable spiritual and natural methods of ministry in the pages of this book before his untimely death.

This book is sure to benefit all people of faith regardless of their present level of spiritual formation. If you would humbly seek more of God's manifestations and spiritual gifts, as described here, I am convinced your life on earth would be transformed by God's kingdom power breaking forth into your life and ministry. Read, enjoy, worship, be challenged, process, write, ask, seek, and demonstrate.

-Thomas Copple
Senior Pastor, Spirit & Truth Worship Center, Orange, CA

Enoch walked with God, and he so pleased God that God took him. So it is with Eli Hernandez who also walked with God, heard His voice, and knew His direction. And, although he has been taken from us, Brother Hernandez has left a gold mine of spiritual insights for us.

This book is an absolute revelation of the workings of the spirit world—and the man who wrote it walked in that Spirit. Like Abel of old, Eli has gone, but he left a road map of how to operate in the spirit world. To me this book is an absolute must read for anyone who desires to walk in the supernatural. My only regret is not having had this great revelation 45 years ago. May God bless these truths to all those who read them.

God's best to you,

- Jeffrey Arnold
Speaker, Author, Retired Pastor,
The Pentecostals of Gainesville, FL

Some books are written to give us information and some books are birthed out of one's passion and insight to impart revelation.

"A World Beyond the Stars" is truly an entrance gate, revealing places in Jesus that have never been imagined!

My dear friend and mentor Eli Hernandez's life and ministry has kept us in awe of the deep, prophetic things of God. And now, with this amazing book, we have a guide to light the way so that we can explore these depths ourselves.

Forward, dear reader. This book is a must have!!!

And may you never be the same!

- Art Wilson
WAFUNIF Goodwill Ambassador and UNMSF Special Advisor
Pastor of The International Church of Metro Detroit

In the span of a generation, God's Spirit calls and then rests upon only a few men in the dimension and power of both authority and anointing as it did on Evangelist Eli Hernandez. His preaching was not focused towards enticing words of man's wisdom but was rather in power and demonstration of the Spirit with revelatory insight and impact. So it is with this penetrating read called, "A World Beyond the Stars." As I read it, I felt like I was with my close friend once again, sharing in and rejoicing over the wisdom from above given to him in abundant, life instructive revelations!

- Marvin Walker
Senior Pastor, Faith Apostolic Church of Troy, MI

Bro. Kenneth Reeves told us that, on rare occasions in life, we would meet someone and our inner spirits would "shake hands." He told us, *that* is a God ordained friendship. So it was, when God graciously connected our spirits to Eli and Kathy's 28 years ago. Although we were close friends, I often longed for Brother Eli to give me a detailed road map to deeper places in the Spirit. HERE IT IS!!

Through Brother Eli's refreshing and unique style of communication, you will be inspired, challenged, and forever changed by the anointing that flows through his written words—just as it did out of his powerful preaching.

- Claudette Walker
Speaker, Ordained Minister of the UPCI

My beginning association with Brother Eli Hernandez goes back many years, when I was Pastor of Life Church, in Anchorage, and Alaska/Yukon District Superintendent (since retired from both). Bro Hernandez stayed in our home, preached at our Church, and blessed us and many others in so many very precious ways.

His sincere attitude towards living for the Lord Jesus was so inspiring to me, as well as to many in our circle of associates.

I encourage the reading of his book, "A World Beyond The Stars," as it reflects so much of his sincerity in his service to the Lord.

Respectfully,

- J. R. Blackshear
Retired Pastor and District Superintendent, Anchorage, Alaska

Evangelist Eli Hernandez -

Seer without peer. Intercessor extraordinaire. Power clothed in humility. Authority by submission. He called me "Bishop" and meant it. Few in our lifetime have walked so closely and constantly attuned to the Spirit realm as Evangelist Eli Hernandez. He walked with God, and God took him. Before he ascended, Bro. Hernandez put pen to paper, imparting key Spiritual and practical principles. While we recognize he was unique, he lamented that—realizing it should not be so. May there be an army of 1 million "Eli Hernandezes" answering the call to operate in the Spirit 24/7/365.

This book, "A WORLD BEYOND THE STARS," is intended to be "caught" rather than "taught." So, don't speed read it—read and reread slowly; study it, absorb it, meditate on it PRAYERFULLY. May it fertilize the seed of purposeful potential God planted in you at new birth to be a Spirit-powered witness to this end-time generation!

Excerpts:

"It is the realm of the Spirit that flows from the throne of God, even as Revelation 22 depicts. Since both anointing and Spirit flow downward, the greatest point of servitude and humility will become the greatest point of saturation."

"[GOD] DOES NOT WANT US MAKING MINISTRIES OUT OF METHODS!"

- Art Hodges III
SoCal District Superintendent, UPCI

Contents

FOREWORD

The loss of Eli Hernandez was a blow to the Apostolic movement. While we may accept the will of God, we are diminished by not having this truly Spiritual preacher of the gospel among us. His ministry will be deeply missed.

Brother Hernandez brought an intensely focused, genuinely passionate Spiritual dimension to his work. Never brash, never self-promoting, he, without fail, put all the attention on Jesus and His Spirit as the source of healing, saving, and delivering. His insights, his sharing of a Word from the Lord as God gave them, was remarkable—and many can testify that Brother Hernandez was used by God to spark their faith, give them hope, and refocus them on God's plan for their lives. His and Sister Hernandez's preaching, praying, and unique worship, brought joy and encouragement to more than we could count.

Even though Brother Hernandez left us far too soon, he—led no doubt by the Holy Ghost—left us a treasure. In this book, "A World Beyond the Stars," this great man of God distilled his understanding and experience in living and ministering in the Spirit of God. Here you will find no-nonsense, down-to-earth instruction and advice on how to walk in the Spirit, and just as important, how to operate in the Spirit in order to lead others into the dimensions of a truly Spiritual life.

In this little book, you will be given a view into the heart of a man who knew this place beyond the stars, explored it, and lived his life to share his discoveries with all of us. The chapter headings alone stir something in us, a lifting of the head and heart, the beginnings of a hunger to go higher, to so walk that we can discover that world: "Bridges," "Unity," "Flow," "Function," "Explore," "New Places," "Expand," and more.

You hold in your hands a true glittering jewel of great value. Read it, absorb it, practice it, and it is not too much to say it holds within it the power to change your life.

Jerry Jones

Professor, Urshan College

ACKNOWLEDGEMENTS

In this world, there are certain people who make things happen. I would be remiss to leave out the people who imparted into my life for this journey to even be possible.

To the Lord Jesus Christ who gave His life and loved me before I knew what love was. Without Him, I can do nothing.

To my dear wife, Kathy, who has been so supportive during times when this book was on the shelf. Her encouragement and backing during those times was just what I needed because of the daunting task ahead of me.

To my daughter, Charity, who—though in her teens—was my perpetual reminder that this book needed to be written. Thank you for continually prompting me to keep this book in front!

Also, to the man of God who was the most influential voice that started me on this journey—Bishop David Elms from Charlotte, NC. I will never forget our lunch when you would not let me go until I committed to write, write, and write! Your push was what I needed to commit to such a task. Without your voice this book would not have occurred! Thank you for being the man of God I needed in that hour!

To my Bishop, Arless Glass, for all the start-up instructions that launched this ministry on the field of evangelism in 1989. I thank God for you and for your endless supply of wisdom and knowledge that has carried us in so many ways over the last thirty years of evangelizing the world!

To my lead editors and subsequent editors … I'm sorry for creating so much work! Debbie Simler-Goff is a jewel in the Kingdom of God! You are a very special person with such a heart for ministry. I pray that God return one-hundred-fold back into your life for the countless hours you spent helping me fine-tune the goals of this writing, and for all the conversations, emails, and journeys we both took to get to this place.

To my follow-up editor, my dear wife, who was willing to take the base writing and finalize the finishing touches. Thank you for making time, between caring for our home, managing our daughter's homeschooling, ministering to ladies all over the country, and caring for me as your husband! Thanks for being an amazing mom and taking on one more thing to make sure this book made sense! Your love for God and your servitude is a priceless treasure to us all!

To the many who have asked me, over and over, "Is the book done?"—Thank you for that constant reminder of what the Lord has asked of me, and, thank you for your patience.

May God bless each of you for the words and motivation that has kept me on the potter's wheel as I journeyed with this project until its completion. It is our desire that God grant you access, wisdom, and strength as you read this book; may it bring you higher than ever before—even into *a world beyond the stars.*

INTRODUCTION

Endeavoring to write a book that creates a path to get into God's divine dimensions is not an easy task. With so much corruption in the world of spiritualism, one has to consider that many religions and faith types have attempted to use anything from meditation to mutilation just to try to get to spiritual places.

Unfortunately, these people have only been able to reach into dimensions of darkness that appear to have a sense of light. Remember, Satan sometimes comes as an angel of light. However, misuse of spiritualism should not become disuse, but rather proper use unto true spirituality.

It is always a fact that false manifestations presuppose the existence of the true and real. Since the devil cannot create, everything he uses comes from the true source of another world that he has copied, corrupted, and misused. These counterfeit manifestations lead people into spiritual dimensions that eventually bring destruction to the mind, body, soul, and spirit.

In these next chapters, we will create short modules with examples of how the Almighty God (even the Lord Jesus Christ) has given us all things in Him, which started in the Spirit.

It is our sincere desire that you find not just an experience of spiritual things (which is what all other forms do) but rather that you find Him (Jesus Christ) and the power of His resurrection and the fellowship of His suffering.

This book will be an entrance gate of how to come into places in Jesus that have never been imagined, by some. I pray that the insight that the Lord has allowed us to experience, over the past thirty years in ministry, will afford each person reading this the necessary revelation to hasten spiritual encounters without fear and failure.

May God grant you the wisdom and strength to accomplish every task set before you as you read and reach for *A World Beyond the Stars*.

CHAPTER ONE

BRIDGES

"His passion to pursue truth led him to exploits beyond his wildest dreams"

In building bridges from earth to heaven, we will reach into realms of spiritual origin in a moment. But first, let us talk about the bridge that must be built by us—not by God. How often have we seen the portrait of God stretching his hand to man—the limp hand of man not even making an effort to touch God?

The first piece of this realm is time-based. What I have noticed in all spiritual journeys attempted by religions and philosophies around the world is that they spend time each day engaging in a path that gets the individual to a certain place in whatever they are trying to reach. Whether it is some inner peace, self-motivation, focal entry, meditation, or other sorts of disciplines, people in general try to enter into something that brings a certain level of satisfaction in spiritual paths.

In a neighborhood we once lived in, there was a man who allowed people to come to his home for "therapy." Oftentimes they would spend two or three days trying to "get rid of things" by standing in one spot (right in front of his house) moving their bodies ever so slightly in order to gain access to the spirit of darkness. What they were practicing is referred to as "tai chi," which comes from another world not known to Christians. It is the process of opening the human spirit to other points of access within the mind, body, spirit, and eventually, the soul. It is amazing how far people will go in order to seemingly "empower" themselves in a moment of solace at the cost of vulnerability and a good feeling.

It is apparent that we are willing to spend time on this flesh and do what we have to, when we have to. We go to the dentist to improve our teeth and spend an hour. We visit the doctor for a check-up, and spend one, two, three hours or more. Some people even sign a waiver and allow themselves to be cut open, hoping to resolve the issue that has caused them to visit the doctor in the first place. We go to the mall to buy one item and sometimes spend up to two hours for what we determine we have need of. Some even take their pets to a vet hospital or groomer and spend several hours going and coming because it pleases their natural state.

Whatever other items (internet, social media, entertainment) that have come to our minds at this point are similar; so many things take up our time, because we have deemed them as necessary.

We say we don't have time for spiritual development, but close calculation reveals that we actually do have time. We honestly don't even need to "make time" for other items in our lives, because of the value attached to them. Therefore, what is needed for a bridge from earth to heaven is value. Whatever we value, we invest in.

If we value the Bible, we will read it.

If we value prayer, we will pray.

If we value God's presence, we will search for Him.

Value is often based on need.

If we get sick, the doctor becomes valuable.

If we get confused, the Bible becomes valuable.

If a crisis occurs, seeking God becomes valuable.

As the need increases, so does the value.

What if higher values could be placed on seeking the supernatural through the knowledge of what has been given to us?

Since we have been made in the image of God, the Spirit Man automatically has an other-world connection, and therefore a natural hungering for the supernatural.

We know that with proper discipline and sound Biblical teaching, there are no limits to the spiritual heights and pathways that God will open to us. But we also know that Satan has corrupted so many into thinking that these things cannot be experienced in a church or atmosphere where Jesus Christ is magnified.

Because of this, people invariably turn what was intended to be spiritual into a religious path or even a denominal path, often filled with misguided and misinformed ideas of how to truly explore the spiritual essence of God. This, in turn, creates the confusion and spiritual crises that are so prevalent in our world today.

The Spirit Man was divinely created to explore spiritual pathways. He craves exploration. He was designed that way by the Spirit of God.

So how do we create a healthy exploratory path to our Lord and Savior without ending up in another confusing spiritual cesspool?

We do so by getting on the right bridge and having the right instruction.

It is necessary during every journey to include a map, idea, or concept. That concept is born out of the hunger for new worlds and/or new dimensions, along with a pursuit that never stops until something is reached.

When Christopher Columbus went out to search for the New World, he was convinced that the world was not flat (as many had believed before him). His passion to pursue truth led him to exploits beyond his wildest dreams. Striving to reach India, he sailed onward until he landed in the Caribbean (later named the "West Indies") in full confidence that he had reached his mark.

Just as Columbus would discover places unknown to him, we also will get to places in God where psychology and much study can never take us.

Some things are taught. There are many Biblically sound books out there to assist in these foundational principals. However, there are also a multiplicity of spiritual principals that can only be caught, and the catching can only be achieved by embarking on the journey without fear, and with proper process. We will never get to places in God higher than where we are unless we build a bridge to the "catching atmosphere."

In order to develop a catching atmosphere in our mind and spirit, we must first seek to build a bridge to the Spirit of God.

In our minds, it is not the God who can heal me, not the God who can supply my needs, not the God who can take care of my family, not the God who can speak answers to my questions, but God Himself—the pure, powerful, holy, majestic, awesome, righteous, creative God!

If we seek God only for what He can do, we will attempt to predicate that on who we are—or perhaps better said, who we are not. We can never get to the Spirit of God that way because the Bible says that "... all have sinned and come short of the glory of God." (Romans 3:23)

So, for starters, let's just seek the presence of Jesus Christ.

I will never forget the question a man who worked at a morgue asked me once.

"Do you know what is spoken in this mortuary, more than anything else?" he asked, a curious look in his eyes, hinting that I should know the answer.

Of course, I wasn't quite sure where he was going with the question, so I answered, "No."

He told me, "It's Jesus. The name of Jesus is used more than any other word spoken in this place."

This brings us to the conclusion that if death carries even the most faithless person to some kind of God consciousness in their logical mind, provoking them to call on the name of Jesus and making them aware of a world beyond, how much more should a spirit-filled believer use the name above all names when seeking to reach the Spirit of God?

Build a bridge by calling the name of Jesus out loud!

Build a bridge by clearing your mind of distracting thoughts.

Build a bridge by immersing yourself into the spiritual realm and allowing the Holy Spirit to take control. We will discuss that further, later in this book.

Just think—that at the mention of His name, "Every knee shall bow and every tongue confess..." (Romans 14:11). For those of us who have spoken His name thousands of times, it may have become second nature to us by now. But there are those in the world who have never even tried to utter the precious name of Jesus. If you are reading this book on a search for spiritual depths, then build a bridge first, using His name.

Demons tremble at the knowledge that God is ONE. God's angels become alert at the sound of the name "Jesus," because it triggers the fear of the Lord, which is where angels dwell. Speak the name of Jesus as it is—the most glorious name you will ever speak! Speak the name of Jesus as the bridge to the greatest dimensions of God. Speak the name of Jesus as the all-inclusive name of God manifested in flesh.

JESUS.

JESUS.

JESUS.

Clear your human spirit by calling on the name of JESUS.

Then, prepare yourself to step onto the bridge that will change everything you know up to this point about a spiritual walk with the living God.

Wait before you read on.

Do you want to read a book or build a bridge to supernatural places in almighty God?

Take some time here and now to call on the name of Jesus, to clear your human spirit, and to build your bridge to the next dimension.

Take more time with Jesus than you do when you are shopping, playing a video game, watching a movie, or visiting a clinic, doctor's office, or hospital. If you will do this, then your personal bridge to the supernatural world will begin to form. You will be on your way to "A World Beyond The Stars."

CHAPTER TWO

PROPER POSITIONS

"Let us remember that resurrection only takes place where dying precedes it."

Once we build our bridge to the supernatural, we can clearly pursue Christ and nothing else. We can pursue Christ, and not our own needs or other agendas. Remember, coming into the King of kings' presence is not about us. Rather, it is entirely about Him.

Whenever human reason stretches to its capacity, the entrance gate of heavenly access becomes available. It is this path which God uses to involve human framework to accomplish His will on the earth, "...just as it is in heaven."

How does an individual gain **access** without fear of failure?

He moves beyond the scope of **textual** proof towards the need for spiritual interaction with the Almighty God.

Some of us have become so accustomed to our current process of reaching to God that we are unaware that we are avoiding **divine operation**.

Once a man or woman reaches a level of spiritual success that is accepted by the general body, he or she can function the rest of his/her days in that realm and never engage in **all** that God has already designed for that individual.

Some call this process "church." Some call it "religion." Some even call it their "denomination." But in reality, it is stagnation—a set of recycled experiences.

Instead of true growth, the "stagnated" believer has become accustomed to a certain level of spiritual interaction and has ceased to move further into the deeper realms of God and His World.

Please don't misunderstand what I am saying. A group of people coming together based on the Holy Scriptures and its fundamental truths is essential for maintaining accountability, structure, strength, and many other powerful segments that we will touch on, later in this book.

The Bible declares it in this manner: *"Not forsaking the assembling of ourselves together… as ye see the day approaching"* (Hebrews 10:25).

In other words, don't miss gathering for church on a weekly basis. It does matter. God designed it that way so we could stay accountable, one toward another.

Regular church attendance, accountability, and submission to spiritual authority are all part of God's plan to keep us balanced and strong as we embark on our supernatural journey.

What I am speaking of here is the danger of just getting our needs met and never realizing the intent of an entirely different lifestyle of the Spirit, in which God intended man to walk.

That spiritual walk is *not* religion. Religion is man's attempt to please God. Of course, this walk is relational, but it is ultimately **spiritual,** because that is the part that touches the eternal realm.

Let us ponder a question at this point, to get a better grip on what hinders us from trying the spirits, as 1 John 4:1-3 instructs:

"Beloved, believe not every spirit, but try the spirits whether they are of God…And every spirit that confesseth not that Jesus Christ is come in the flesh is not of God…"

Are we afraid of what we have never been taught to exercise? Are we frightened by what can get out of control? Are we locked inside parameters that have ruled our stagnation and now we have become accustomed to what we know, instead of searching the deep things of God?

As it is described in the Bible, in 1 Corinthians, chapter 2, there are deep things that can go even further into hidden wisdom. This hidden wisdom is then said to develop, even to unsearchable riches in Ephesians 3 ... unless of course, they are revealed. How would they be revealed? "BY THE SPIRIT!"

Truth was a person before it was a doctrine, for Jesus Christ said, *"...I am the way, the truth..."* (John 14:6).

Take time here to meditate on that last statement for a few minutes.

Repeat it.

"Truth was a person before it was a doctrine."

Continue this process until it begins to metabolize and the depth and the knowledge of this Truth reverberates through your spirit into your soul chamber. Then allow it to re-ignite your Apostolic, spiritual passion.

We, in the 21st Century, need to return to our Apostolic roots of the Book of Acts and become as Apostolic in function as we are in foundation and form.

I realize this type of writing will challenge and even open the door for criticism. However, at this point in my life, the Spirit of God has so arrested me that I must write these things unto you.

It has become just as essential for me to speak what "thus saith the Lord" in this end time as it was for the Apostle Paul in his time.

Let's probe into the realm of divine operation by first creating the process designed by God himself and exercised in His earthly ministry.

It has become obvious by the Bible's New Testament that the process of Jesus Christ was one to be repeated over and over to gain proper access into the heavenly things freely given to us by divine operation. 1 Corinthians 2:12 states, *". . . that we might know the things that are freely given to us of God."*

The first realm of understanding stems back to the entrance in Jerusalem, where Jesus cleansed the temple. In John's writing, the author addresses the approach to the process of entering the established temple and approaching the rulers to accomplish two basic things.

The first objective was to remove the created "in-house" stigma that had now vexed the Pharisees and caused vendors to come inside the courts, shutting off all access to the outer courts—where the less fortunate were supposed to have access to worshipping God.

The outer court was a place where the lame, blind, and halt people had access to at least worship God, purchase their sacrifices, and give adoration to their creator.

That had all been removed, because the vendors had realized how much gain could be had from inside the temple, along with a higher value system from those who were allowed inside. Of course, the price they would receive for those sacrifices would also be greater.

When the Lord saw that, he made cords to beat those *inside* the house —NOT those *outside* the house.

Let's be careful what we beat—if we beat anything at all. They are His sheep, and not ours. We are just managers in this Kingdom, not owners.

Now that the temple was cleansed, Jesus could once again give access to the less fortunate (His second objective). Matthew records that, after this, the lame, blind, halt, etc. came to Jesus and He healed them of their diseases.

Perhaps the reason that we don't have access is because we have a closed court and a pricy temple. Let us reopen the doors for the lame and blind to have access, and perhaps it won't be so hard to get to where the miracles always happen.

Once Jesus had given them access, it wasn't the priests and the Pharisees who received His ministry. Instead, the sick people who needed a physician or healer the most received the Lord's ministry.

So, in our initial approach to access, we have a cleansing. This bears the similar marks of our great redemption plan as well.

Repent.

That is what Isaiah saw in Isaiah 41, prior to the Kingdom of Heaven that would be at hand. Thus it behooves us to keep repentance as a preliminary process rather than just a moment to get forgiveness.

It appears to me that, after thirty years of traveling the world and ministering amongst churches which are at various levels of utilizing the five-fold ministry (apostles, prophets, evangelists, pastors and teachers) that I have seen many forgo the entry level of repentance.

Instead, repentance is used as the resource for receiving forgiveness. Though repentance does bring about forgiveness, according to the Holy Scriptures, it does much more than that. We must understand that repentance is not just the element used for coming to God—rather, repentance is a constant position that needs to be exercised daily.

The Apostle Paul said he died *daily*.

Let us remember that resurrection only takes place where dying precedes it. Therefore, let us die to resurrect. It is not the dying that Paul enjoyed, but he understood that every process of dying in Jesus Christ produced a resurrection.

Death before resurrection is one point, but let us continue in this vein just a bit more.

The process of repentance, according to Mark chapter one, reveals much more than just forgiveness. Let's examine what transpired when Jesus was baptized by John the Baptist in Jordan:

1.) The heavens opened.

2.) The Spirit descended.

3.) There was a voice.

Let's build a bridge. In this exercise we will go through a process of the mind, body, and spirit.

First is the MIND.

Let's take the mind through the process of emptying ourselves. *"God, here I am with my frailties, failures, and futile attempts. Please forgive me of me."*

Second is the BODY.

"God, I give the actions of my flesh to you. Every way that has not been pleasing in your sight, I give to you." (Whatever comes to your thought process during this prayer, give it to God and clear the physical path of habits that you can't seem to stop.)

Third is the SPIRIT.

In this action, shut everything and everyone out. Concentrate only on the One True God, Jesus Christ. Now open your mouth and speak what He is giving you. (The entry point to receiving the Holy Ghost is similar to the process of gaining access to divine operation in every other spiritual dimension we desire.)

Let's walk through the process listed above.

"The heavens opened." The first chapter of Mark describes something worth noticing. Throughout the Old Testament, the heavens are not shown as being opened—except for a supernatural moment in Ezekiel 1:1, when Ezekiel saw the heavens opened and visions from God. Other than that, there are only references to the *"heavens spread," "heavens created," "heavens declared,"* but no access to an "open heaven" is noted.

However, when you get to Mark 1 and Jesus is submerged in John the Baptist's baptism, which, as we know, is the baptism of repentance, he comes out of the water—and the immediate response is that "...the heavens opened."

"And straightway coming up out of the water, he saw the heavens opened, and the Spirit like a dove descending upon him" (Mark 1:10).

However, the crisis we have created is that those in the church have become accustomed to repenting only when things get "bad enough"—instead of repenting daily, for heavenly access.

I perceive that the enemy has done this to us and has blinded our eyes to the path of access in the heavenly realm. Once access is gained, the Kingdom of God truly is at hand—as long as we stay repented and humbled through the process.

It is no wonder that Jesus used this baptism as the initial action prior to His miraculous ministry, in order to allow those things from heaven to validate His next three years.

Would it be possible for us to engage, as a body, in the daily habit of dying through repentance and entering into humility?

Maybe that would also remove the arrogance and pride that has infested the body of believers, because of the level of knowledge we now have.

Pride never considers repenting daily.

Arrogance never considers repenting daily.

Self-righteousness never considers repenting daily.

I will leave that for pondering, as I do not presume to have anything save Jesus and His crucifixion.

It is our responsibility to seek to die daily, so that the enemy won't have an advantage through pride.

As the Bible declares, *"Pride goeth before destruction, and an haughty spirit before a fall"* (Proverbs 16:18).

I remember a story once told by the late, esteemed, Reverend Billy Cole. He said that there was a man who preached a message and was feeling bad for doing less than what he knew he could do.

(We must be careful that the art of preaching not consume us, lest the anointing can't lead us. We must study to show ourselves approved—absolutely—but, according to the fourth chapter of Luke, we must be anointed if we are to preach.)

In this story, the man was telling Bishop Cole that he was sorry for not doing a better job preaching that day's message.

Bishop Cole then turned and said, "I rebuke that spirit of pride."

The man who had preached was shocked by Bishop Cole's response, and began to explain that he only mentioned it because he knew that he could have done better.

Bishop Cole then replied, "If you take credit for doing bad, you will take credit for doing good! We must do the best we can, and leave the rest up to God!"

Regarding church services, I have seen, on many occasions, a great thought come forth; something no one has ever heard was preached. The entire congregation deemed that as success—yet there was no supernatural movement.

What happened? Was it God who revealed that message?

I would not dare dabble in that thought, as only God and that person would know that.

However, I will say that (as I have witnessed in this situation) the minister, in that moment, often didn't know how to flow in the supernatural. He was not able to bring the body into the realm where that preached Word would have been able to take deep root. Soil is only as moist as the amount of moisture that flows to it. If the Spirit is related to water, as it is in the Word of God, then moisture becomes the requirement for "stickability" in order for the preached Word of God to adhere to the souls of men. Singing does not accomplish that—prayer does! That is why we have altar services. The altar should be the place where deep prayer follows the Word spoken, so the Word can remain—planted deep within each soul.

So, when seeking heavenly direction at the altar call of a church service, remember these two things:

1. Begin with a spirit of repentance.
2. Nurture the moisture of God's Spirit, to a point of engaging in the Spirit while the supernatural is open to the entire body.

The average altar service has been timed at only seven minutes—but we can change that paradigm.

Let us fall on our faces once again and repent, that God may grant us access into realms that have been waiting on us.

Let me offer these exercises regarding spiritual application, so everyone—from leaders, all the way through the entire body—may engage every time we come together.

Since individual faith has its limits (because an individual prays within the parameters of their own knowledge base) perhaps a lesson on corporate prayer is applicable here, in order to help the body of Christ to become more productive in these last days.

In the early church, throughout the book of Acts, great moves of God influenced the entire church body, even to the point where prison doors were opened by an angel sent from God.

It would do the church of today much good, to engage in like manner as a body in every single service, prayer meeting, and function we have together.

According to Leviticus 26:8, *"And five of you shall chase an hundred, and an hundred of you shall put ten thousand to flight..."* therefore, what could a church of 100, 200, 300 people, 500, or 5000 or more do? Only the Spirit of God knows that—but it must be huge.

Let's engage the body of Christ and see what God will do. (If God can't manage His church, then we sure can't.) Allow His operation of divine moments to be recognized, and give an opportunity for God's Spirit to move every time His church gets together. At least we will begin a process, or function, that will give us dimensions like never before.

Remember that faith cannot operate where fear is nurtured. Do not allow the fear from the enemy to convince you that spiritual movement is not necessary. Throughout the book of Acts, good preaching alone did not bring revival; it was accompanied by a divine move of the Spirit of God. And, if divine movement was necessary for Jesus, it's necessary for the church today.

Let's exercise an entrance here with repentance.

(If you are having trouble finding something to repent about, refer to Proverbs 6:16 and the "...six things doth the Lord hate: yea, seven are an abomination unto him." Or, If that's not sufficient, go to Proverbs 8:13 where he describes the things we are to hate, if we are to fear the Lord.)

Let's take some time to repent right now. Entertain God's presence—access an "open heaven."

CHAPTER THREE

UNITY

"We did not pray for revival. We prayed for unity and revival came!" – Teklemariam Gezahagne

Now that *access* is gained, we step over into *function* as the Lord leads us. What function?

According to Ephesians 4:16, *"From whom the whole body fitly joined together and compacted by that which every joint supplieth, according to the effectual working in the measure of every part, maketh increase of the body unto the edifying of itself in love."*

The supply and increase that comes from God and moves through the body of Christ is dependent on unity. Just as repentance is the act (or function) of getting us into God's presence, unity is the act of keeping us there.

Dimension-changing unity can only be acquired through faith and repentance. If you desire to experience this operation within the church body, then Biblical unity must be fully operational at every level and in every church service.

The Bible requires us to work hard in order to keep the body of Christ together through the unity of the faith. When unity is functioning properly, as the scripture says (in Ephesians 4:16), two things begin to happen: (1) There is supply, and (2) there is increase. When a church is perfectly unified, any member of the body has access to that supply, which becomes available through the operation of the Spirit. At this point, increase is automatic because the nature of God *is* unity. When the church binds together, its growth is inevitable.

Unfortunately, unity has been replaced in our churches with a few functional members rather than the entire body. It appears that we have become satisfied with a just few people who can operate in the gifts of the Spirit, removing the need for the body to work together as one. Paul makes this reference in 1 Corinthians 14:39, when he says, "Wherefore, brethren, covet to prophesy, and forbid not to speak with tongues."

The object here is not that everyone should prophesy; rather, that everyone in the church should engage in some type of spiritual movement and not depend on a mere few.

Let's take a journey. Now that we are engaged in the spirit by the right approach (as mentioned in Chapter 2), it is time to delve into the process of using the body (speaking of the church body) correctly.

First, we must release God's people and give them liberty to operate in the Spirit. (Please note that I am only referencing people who are faithfully living for God at home as well as in the church.)

At this point, those reading should already be on a path to spiritual things. Paul said it best in 1 Corinthians 14:1, "Follow after charity, and desire spiritual gifts." It's time to move from desiring spiritual gifts to working in the Spirit.

It has become obvious to me that "much learning" can harden us. In other words, one can know how to preach well, but can then struggle to operate well in the Spirit. For instance, if you look at Acts chapter ten, Peter knew what to do while he was preaching. He was sensitive to the wind of the Holy Ghost when it brushed over the congregation.

Being sensitive to these movements becomes imperative when going beyond—just preaching a message. Let's take a look at Acts 10:44, *"While Peter yet spake these words, the Holy Ghost fell on all them which heard the word."*

What I find interesting here, is that it never shows us where Peter finished his message. He was interrupted. But he knew what to do, and how to flow with the Spirit. When he allowed the Spirit to move, everyone in the room received the Holy Ghost and was baptized in Jesus' name.

The same relational point is valid in any other movement of the Spirit—and we need to know what to do and how to flow in it. We relegate the initial moves of the Spirit to shouting, dancing, running, and such like. Now, please don't misinterpret me here; I love a church that engages in those things—but those actions are human entry points. Those moments are signals indicating where we need to go—and that has the potential to become, what I call, "body ministry."

True and effective body ministry is where each person has a "Spirit-supply" that they have developed, personally—and that supply becomes magnified through corporate faith, when the body of believers assemble.

When the body is connected by operating in true body ministry, the powerful effects of the unity of the Spirit—one voice, one mind, and one sound—comes into play. At that point, it becomes the entry point for all spiritual movements, as in Acts chapter 2.

"And when the day of Pentecost was fully come, they were all with one accord in one place. And suddenly there came a sound from heaven as of a rushing mighty wind, and it filled all the house where they were sitting" (Acts 2:1-2).

I remember a statement that forever changed my thinking—and perhaps it will affect yours.

I was pondering the great revival I had seen while in Africa. I was sure that much prayer had been made to get to this place—but how they prayed was what piqued my curiosity.

When I asked the man of God, "How did you pray to have such great revival and such a powerful move of God?" he answered, "We did not pray for revival, we prayed for unity and revival came!"

Do we really understand the components of unity?

I dare say not, or we would strive every day to bring the body together, that the function of unity would have its greatest affect when we join together—every time.

Please understand that I am very aware of our human response—to *not* be introspective, but rather to excuse ourselves, (or excuse me) of not having the experience to make such statements.

However, if the scripture is true, then we must look at Psalms 133, where brethren dwell in unity (as the basis for such thoughts as listed above).

Psalm 133:1 exemplifies (illustrates) this best:

"Behold, how good and how pleasant it is for brethren to dwell together in unity!"

Just "good" and "pleasant" alone could be sufficient reason for seeking to attain unity.

However, I believe the greatest component here is "TO DWELL."

Dwell?

That is a state of living. We call our homes dwelling places. It's the place we know so well that we could practically walk around the rooms blindfolded.

Are we able to do that in unity? Visiting unity when we need its benefits is not the same as dwelling in unity. We must learn to dwell.

Why?

Because God already knew that once we could dwell in unity, the body effect of ministry would take off—and the impossible would now become possible.

Thus the reason why the message of ONE GOD has become so crucial ... it is all wrapped around unity.

GOD IS ONE!

The understanding of the "Oneness of God" is the greatest dimension of unity that exists anywhere. It is the only function that allows the church to be in full force—and not have a gap where the enemy can get in.

The only way to maintain such a level is through repentance. Perhaps that is the reason that arrogance and pride have vexed some churches—to keep the body ministry, and unity, out of the church at large.

Now, Ephesians the 4th chapter leads us down the path of an equally supplied body:

(4) There is one body, and one Spirit, even as ye are called in one hope of your calling;

(5) One Lord, one faith, one baptism,

(6) One God and Father of all, who is above all, and through all, and in you all.

(7) But unto every one of us is given grace according to the measure of the gift of Christ.

(8) Wherefore he saith, When he ascended up on high, he led captivity captive, and gave gifts unto men.

(9) (Now that he ascended, what is it but that he also descended first into the lower parts of the earth?

(10) He that descended is the same also that ascended up far above all heavens, that he might fill all things.)

(11) And he gave some, apostles; and some, prophets; and some, evangelists; and some, pastors and teachers;

(12) For the perfecting of the saints, for the work of the ministry, for the edifying of the body of Christ:

(13) Till we all come in the unity of the faith, and of the knowledge of the Son of God, unto a perfect man, unto the measure of the stature of the fulness of Christ:

(14) That we henceforth be no more children, tossed to and fro, and carried about with every wind of doctrine, by the sleight of men, and cunning craftiness, whereby they lie in wait to deceive;

(15) But speaking the truth in love, may grow up into him in all things, which is the head, even Christ:

(16) From whom the whole body fitly joined together and compacted by that which every joint supplieth, according to the effectual working in the measure of every part, maketh increase of the body unto the edifying of itself in love.

Verses 4-6 immediately establish ONE thing—Everything comes out of ONENESS. The word "ONE" is mentioned seven times in three verses.

Nothing else is so emphatically established as this, in the Word of God.

Ephesians talks about the body—not just the body but ONE BODY—one body with many components.

Now let's discuss components like arms, legs, feet, hands, eyes, ears, nose, mouth, and touch ... the senses! How can the church operate without body function?

It cannot.

Otherwise, the church body would become an island, which would be isolated and opened to the devil's destruction. Isolation and self-operation are the devil's playground for destruction, because there is no unity with God's Spirit.

Again, Ephesians chapter 4 mentions a place where every person has a supply and/or a gift of grace, according to the measure of Christ—which is the operational part of body ministry. Because every person in the body of Christ matters, what they give and take also matters.

Once true Apostolic body ministry is established, we can move on into function. Without getting into further detail (that would be a book in itself), let us move to the next chapter, where flow begins to process through the body and supplies to each section or body part.

CHAPTER FOUR

FLOW

When the body comes into the dimension of unity, the heavenly realm opens and things begin to flow out of the throne of God, and not just from a personal, intellectual, or textual realm.

It is the realm of the Spirit that flows from the throne of God, even as Revelation 22 depicts. Since both anointing and Spirit flow downward, the greatest point of servitude and humility will become the greatest point of saturation.

As the body begins to serve one another, something else is released in the atmosphere of God. At this point, we have disengaged from self-service, and engaged in the service of others.

The greatest realm comes into being at this point. Let's look at Matthew's writings, in reference to that statement. "Greatest of all" is the realm that Jesus talked about, when the disciples were seemingly tugging for position. However, Jesus steps in at that moment and secures, that the way of His Kingdom would be different than that of the Gentiles. What is the way of the Gentiles? It is the competitive, self-indulgent, self-caring, and self-receiving realm which the church seems to engross themselves in on a constant basis. I am quite shocked how the body can perpetually be so in-tune with the events happening all around it, and non-sensitive to the movements of the Spirit—except when they are in a church service. Perhaps our humility is based on what we need? Or, is it based on thanksgiving for what He has done? I don't believe we can know humility in ourselves, because the moment we think we are humble, we no longer are. However, as Peter described the action, let us constantly cast our care upon Him to keep HIM enthroned, thus casting our crowns daily before him.

Matthew 18:4 *Whosoever therefore shall humble himself as this little child, the same is greatest in the kingdom of heaven.*

From leadership to saints, we are infested with taking care of ourselves. Let us delve into the realm of Acts chapter 4, where they—the church—had need of nothing.

Acts 4:32 *And the multitude of them that believed were of one heart and of one soul: neither said any of them that ought of the things which he possessed was his own; but they had all things common.*

(33) And with great power gave the apostles witness of the resurrection of the Lord Jesus: and great grace was upon them all.

(34) Neither was there any among them that lacked: for as many as were possessors of lands or houses sold them, and brought the prices of the things that were sold,

(35) And laid them down at the apostles' feet: and distribution was made unto every man according as he had need.

I find that we still struggle with the realm of "others" and consider ourselves successful when we have outreach once or twice a week. The rest of our energies are most often reserved for ourselves.

Let's look at our structure, and let's be honest with what comes over the pulpits on a perpetual basis. Here is what we are hearing: "Pray for my aunt, mom, dad, daughter, son, family, etc." Yes—and just to balance things out—we include the world at times. However, what if theory of "self" was waived and the principle of "others" was the predominant factor with this understanding: If we serve others, God will take care of our needs? Rare thought process—and thus the reason for our request types. We actually don't believe that if we take care of others God will handle our needs, according to His ability to do exceeding and abundantly ... or do we? We are asking the question, not as though we have attained.

Allow me to insert a personal story here that resulted in amazing miracles for a nine-week period. We traveled to San Jose, CA, and were scheduled for one Sunday; we were there to minister in two services—both a morning and an evening service. By Sunday night, people's faith had risen to a level that Spiritual operation and function were flowing clearly. I felt impressed to engage the body in ministry.

I had been teaching the principle of serving others for about a year, from place to place. The way I was led by the Lord's Spirit was this: "Find two people who need a miracle. Have one person pray for the other—then ask the person who *did* the praying—not the one who was prayed for—how they were feeling." So, I would call on two people who had the same type of sickness or disease. I would ask one to pray for the other's healing. After prayer had taken place, I asked the person who had been *doing* the praying how *they* were feeling. Often times, the strange look of ... "We weren't praying for me, but for ..."—right at that moment, tears, shock, joy would hit, when they realized that while they were serving someone else in the Spirit—they were being healed.

On this occasion, in San Jose, I had no idea that the person God directed me to *do* the praying had severe problems. He had a bullet stuck in his body, too close to his lungs for the doctors to remove. Eventually—within a period of three years—cancer had begun to grow around that bullet, and he was in constant pain. So, in this church service, after he prayed for someone else, I asked him to check his own body and see how he felt. When he realized that he no longer had pain anywhere in his body, he started running around the building—and the entire church congregation erupted in dancing, shouting, praise, and prayer!

By this time, the pastor and I had already decided we would continue the meeting—and neither of us had any idea that the meeting would continue for nine weeks. God did amazing things! But what we discovered, just a few days later, was the tremendous miracle that *actually* happened that first Sunday. You see, later that week, the man with the bullet in his chest, who was healed, called the pastor with a victory report. He said that the doctor had checked him out—and the doctor insisted on testing him again, and again, and again. The doctor finally came out to speak to the man, and said, "It doesn't bother me that I can't find the cancer! What's bothering me is that I can't find the bullet, and I can't find the hole!"

Remember that our subject is serving others. I wonder what would happen if we, while walking in the Spirit of Jesus Christ our Lord, would serve others on a constant basis; our prayers would be surrounded with the passion for others to receive miracles, signs, and wonders. In the story above, that miracle started a meeting that resulted in over 100 people filled with God's Spirit speaking with tongues—and some 250 miracles, of which eight documented cancers were removed! Also, a woman with scoliosis from her birth, and in her thirties, with an "S-curved spine" was made straight and could now walk normal!

Now, let's get back to Jesus' reference of His Kingdom. Which was the "greatest" reference? That of becoming a servant to *most*? No, it was of being a servant to *all*. Please don't misunderstand me as saying that we must be a *slave* to all—because a slave has little or no relationship. But a servant builds something over time. This concept in God's Kingdom was for the purpose of positioning. One leads to another, until we become heirs, according to Galatians. Then our position with Christ culminates back to its original foundation, when we are judged in the end, to hear him say, "Well done thou good and faithful SERVANT."

What a process! Being a servant of the Lord positions us in so many ways, that it becomes necessary— both throughout our present salvation, on an everyday basis, and then bringing us to the end of salvation, where we will be with the Lord for eternity.

It's a positional thing with God and the Spirit-world we live in. As far as the devil is concerned, we are no more hidden than our level of servitude. Once that element of humility is taken away (or left by us, that we might get "noticed") we lose that celestial connection. How? Our level of being a servant to others keeps right posture in the presence of people and in the presence of God. And truly, Jesus was hidden, for the Bible declares in 1 Corinthians 2:6, *"Howbeit we speak wisdom among them that are perfect: yet not the wisdom of this world, nor of the princes of this world, that come to nought:*

(7) But we speak the wisdom of God in a mystery, even the hidden wisdom, which God ordained before the world unto our glory:

(8) Which none of the princes of this world knew: for had they known it, they would not have crucified the Lord of glory."

Then it goes on to tell us of all the things that are revealed by the Spirit, just because of a simple action to serve in humility—where everything in God's Kingdom flows.

If somehow we could maintain that posture, we would have perpetual access to what flows through us—and not just what flows to us.

It's the conduit versus the cistern concept. Cisterns were used as the reserve, in old times, in case of war, and it became the preservation and not the supply. The danger of a cistern is, we withhold enough to maintain ours and our own. With a conduit, you never hold anything back, because of the constant flow from another source—and you freely give to others, making sure that the conduit remains the conduit. There is no need for reserve, since that which is flowing is always fresh, new, and powerful, with constant movement!

Others is the only way a servant maintains freshness. It appears that men and woman of God serve, but at a certain point may easily forget the concept of remaining a servant, losing the flow and thus surviving as cisterns.

God help us humble ourselves, again and again, that we may stay connected to the source that provides fresh flow every day!

Question: When was the last time you prayed in the Spirit? When was the last time you were so lost in the Spirit, that you forgot everything around you that had you worried—about bills, size of congregation, who's leaving, and who's coming? When was the last time God was able to purify you with His flow?

Can we fall on our faces once again, and remember whence we came and who we were meant to serve in the first place? It's—HIM! Let's serve HIM with gladness! Then, every other service is with gladness also.

CHAPTER FIVE
FUNCTION

How to walk above the stars and keep your feet on the ground.

Where is the balance of the spiritual, versus the natural realm where we live?

That must be the age-old question that every pastor, saint, and person who has ever engaged with God has asked, at some point in their walk with Him.

We've all heard statements such as:

- He's so heavenly minded that he's no earthly good.
- He has his head in the clouds.
- She's so spiritual no one can talk to her.
- He is always hearing from God; can God talk to one man that much?

I am sure that the list goes on and on in your circle of influence. Suffice it to say, we really need some applicable scriptural helps to keep us from fearing those dimensions—due to not having process that is scripturally based.

When I think of "spiritual," I think of someone who, first of all, has the Spirit of God. Let's talk about Peter, since he was at Pentecost and was filled with the Spirit of God speaking in other tongues, as we are today. That is the evidence of His Spirit in us—not to be confused with Corinthians, where the operation of the "gift of tongues" is mentioned for a different operation in the body of Christ.

Everyone needs the Spirit of God with the evidence of speaking in tongues. It's Jesus' explanation to Nicodemus in John chapter three, of being born of water (which is our baptism by immersion in Jesus' name), and being born of the Spirit (that's receiving the Holy Spirit speaking in other tongues, or words and sounds that are not from our natural state). Also, it's a cultural thing. In the culture of Heaven, it's super-normal to speak in a heavenly language. In order to stay on our topic, I will leave this matter of essence here and just say, ask the Lord once to fill you with His Spirit and then worship in faith. Don't ask again—just receive—and in just a few moments you will begin to speak utterances with your tongue and mouth that are from Heaven. (If you don't believe, don't worry, it won't happen!) I speak to you with the experience of seeing over half a million people receive this experience, over the last 30 years, and in over 50 countries. All of them spoke in a heavenly language, which was not learned, but rather given by the Spirit of God flowing through them. Let's move on now to the effect this had on the apostle Peter's life.

When Peter was filled with the Holy Spirit, he was infused with the potential to enter into realms beyond human comprehension. Though some may contend that they have had spiritual experiences without speaking in tongues, I am addressing living in this realm with your feet planted on the ground.

Now Peter, in Acts chapter ten of the Holy Bible, was about to eat dinner. Wait! Let's stop right there! He was what? Ok, let us read it for ourselves.

Acts 10:9 *"On the morrow, as they went on their journey, and drew nigh unto the city, Peter went up upon the housetop to pray about the sixth hour:*

(10) And he became very hungry, and would have eaten: but while they made ready, he fell into a trance,

(11) And saw heaven opened, and a certain vessel descending unto him, as it had been a great sheet knit at the four corners, and let down to the earth:"

Even things that are revealed in Heaven, according to verse 11, have the ability to be released or "let down to earth." However, what gets my attention more than anything is the fact that Peter was really just waiting for dinner to be cooked and served—just like a person who has come home from work and is waiting for his wife to make dinner, and has taken a moment to pray in their upper chamber.

What I believe causes the initial statements—like the statements posed at the beginning of this chapter—of high-mindedness or the like, is the fact that most people don't see this as something that can be accessed by just praying before dinner is served. They see reaching those arenas by some powerful prayer meeting or corporate faith moment, with many people engaged in an attempt to reach something great through these moments. I am not suggesting that's not possible, for truly that has happened as well, but our purpose here is to cause that same kind of awareness that is maintained in those types of settings to now translate into the common, everyday setting and life of a typical workday. After heading home, instead of picking up the newspaper or turning on the TV, go to your upper chamber and fall into a trance via the Holy Ghost moving and—the next thing you know—God steps into your cultural world and brings His heavenly culture into operation.

In that light, let's discuss reaching for dimensions as such without fearing that we might go off the deep end.

How is that possible? Let me present a few options here for starters.

1) **Connected.** We must stay connected to the Lord Jesus Christ, where spiritual movements become as normal as conversing with your neighbor. I DID NOT SAY AS CASUAL AS— because this is supernatural—but NOT SPOOKY either. This divine operation is not some mystical, dark side, divination act of spiritual chaos that doesn't make sense. It has order, because God is not the author of confusion. He is *"the author and finisher of our faith"*—which does bring us into unknown realms that are scripturally, and spiritually, sound.

2) **Conscious**. We must stay aware, because it could be morning, night, or noon. We must STOP relegating these types of visitations to a conference, church service, or some other special type of

meeting. We must learn how to integrate awareness into our daily lives by cutting out the distractions that take up those moments. THINK ABOUT THE FACT THAT GOD USED A VERY NON-CHURCH SETTING TO RELEASE A VISION ABOUT THE GREATEST REVIVAL IN THE WORLD!!! We would not want to miss that! Becoming more aware may cost us some internet time, video game time, talk radio show time, sports time, and the list goes on. I'm not suggesting giving up those items, if that's your choice. What I'm speaking of here is learning to be conscious enough to be able to stop in the middle of what we are doing, no matter how engaged we are, and still have the ability to hear, see, feel, and function at that exact moment when God wants to use us.

Example—it's the fourth quarter of your favorite team's game; they are about to win with a field goal, there are only ten seconds left in the game, God steps in, and He says, "Turn it off and pray!" Are you struggling with this scenario—or whatever scenario you may set yourself in? Perhaps it's something other than a game—but the point is the same. If your mind said, "Uh, I'm not sure if I could" or "That would be hard" (or some other rational), that's why you haven't had many moments like Peter. Let's stop here for a moment, lift our hands, and ask God to turn our hearts, eyes, ears, and minds toward Him, that we may become more conscious. When you're done praying, we will continue.

3) **Exercised.** Peter was very hungry when this vision came to him, while in a trance—as the Bible clearly states. (Trance is mentioned four other times in the Bible, with some asleep and some awake). He had to make a decision to acquiesce to his flesh or let the Spirit have its way. QUESTION: Would you have dismissed it and eaten? Peter had to make a willing decision to step into what God was showing him, even though his cultural upbringing was fighting him the entire time, until he finally gave in. It's obvious to me that he had the ability to choose while in the Spirit. He told The Lord, "No—unclean!" three times, and even doubted in himself about what he just saw, before he said, "Ok, ok, I'll do it." When the door

was answered, and Cornelius's servants were at the door, he had no problem receiving GENTILES!

What? Gentiles? He was able to function and exercise the will of God because he was in the Spirit first. I wonder what would have happened had Peter not had a trance/vision to help him deal with the Gentiles who ended up spending the night in a Jewish household—which is yet another miracle in itself. We must be willing to engage when the Spirit moves, whether in our homes, cars, job, market, or wherever God chooses. He knows we work; he gave us our jobs. Perhaps, many times, God waits because we don't live our lives with properly prepared environments, and God can't speak. Or, maybe we are not exercising holy environments, filled with His Spirit, and thus we have to wait until we get to church—because it's the only place we entertain the Holy Ghost? I pray that's not the case in your life!

4) **Responsive.** After we get visitations like that, what we do with them is just as important as having them. Sometimes people have become so overwhelmed by the visitation that they have missed the point. God does not reveal himself to get us excited! He has process and destiny in every vision, dream, trance, and out-of-body experience that is encountered. And, these experiences are usually not just for you! They usually will affect more than just your needs, wants, ministry, or anything else that may be centered around self. God is wanting to use you—don't ruin it! Peter was responsive to what God said because he was willing to obey, even though it went against his tradition. He was now going to receive Gentiles into his home! Then, he would eventually go to the Gentiles! I'm sure some of those around him thought he had lost his mind.

Let me interject here, that, when something is given by God, IT WILL NEVER CONTRADICT THE HOLY BIBLE because it's still HIM! If it does—IT WAS NOT GOD—NO MATTER WHAT!

That being said, let me move onto exercising Spiritual moments with Jesus. Why do we perceive that the greatest moments will happen in Spiritual atmospheres that *we* view as great—like, when

1,000 or 10,000 people gather together. Why not begin realizing that in a normal day, with your feet planted in normal settings like work, school, or even during your daily workout, while your feet are planted, we can become very sensitive to His movements. It has happened that way so many times in our lives that we can't possibly count the times. I perceive that many times the Lord was ready to give us such a moment, but we were too busy trying to solve, answer, give our opinion, fix it, or some other self-propelled action, that we actually missed His action. I, for one, have done so more than once, and have learned it would have been different had I become more aware.

So, to review this assessment and chapter, let us reiterate two things that stand out to us, as we ponder our ability to walk in the Spirit: Awareness and activity. Both of these require a change in our lifestyle. We all have become so busy that God is boxed into speaking to us when we have a need or when we are in a corporate spiritual setting, where it is convenient. WE MUST STOP THIS! Turn off your media, turn off your series, turn off your talk show—or whatever is getting in the way of awareness! God is trying to talk to us and visit us in ways we have not even fathomed! Once we hear, then we can activate what He is saying and perhaps have the greatest revival that has ever been in our town, state, province, nation, and world!

Then you move into, "What do I do with what I have experienced?" DON'T JUST TELL EVERYONE YOU SEE!! Ask God for wisdom! **James 1:5,** *"If any of you lack wisdom, let him ask of God, that giveth to all men liberally, and upbraideth not; and it shall be given him."*

Wisdom is the "how to" of visions, dreams, trances, and out-of-body experiences! Everything that has happened to the writer will never fully be told in public—it's not wise to cast your pearls before the swine! And, unfortunately, there are some "pigs" among us! We must use wisdom, lest pride, arrogance, confusion, fear, doubt, contention, or disunity would attempt to get in the way of a heavenly moment and cause delays in what God has in store for those who love Him.

These are simply entry points to learning "how to"—with our feet on the ground—knowing that at any moment, the Spirit that moves without a time clock may want to use us for His glory—and not ours!

CHAPTER SIX
FAILURE

Taking steps: TRY THE SPIRITS AND SEE!

Up to this point, we have only discussed the positive aspects of reaching upward into the realms of God's world and being able to live decent, Godly lives at the same time.

However, knowing the Bible and the letters to the church at Corinth, one learns that there will be mistakes in the process of growing into maturity, by exercising what is given to us freely.

As the Bible says:

1 John 4:1 *"Beloved, believe not every spirit, but try the spirits whether they are of God: because many false prophets are gone out into the world."*

So, this passage leads us to know that there are false prophets! Watch out, because they are out there! So, is everyone who is used by God, and makes a mistake, a false prophet—or, do they automatically fall into that category? I would think not, because then we *all* are—because NO ONE reading this book has lived their life without a mistake or sin. As it says in **Romans 3:23**, *"For all have sinned, and come short of the glory of God."*

So then, how do we separate the difference? There is a big difference between a FALSE prophet and a MISTAKEN prophet—or, for the purpose of teaching here, let's use "person" since we are not all prophets here. What's the difference? MOTIVES! That was the difference between King David and King Saul—MOTIVES! Right motives and right spirits in the operation of the Spirit of God will go much further than all the ill motives in the world! GOD KNOWS THE HEART!

Perhaps people start with right motives, but then something gets in the way. What is that "something"? I see a pattern for right motives turned wrong. In King Saul's case, there are two aspects that brought about a motive change in his actions and heart. I think the first and most obvious is his altar—or lack of it. It doesn't appear that Saul had very many recorded altars of his own. It does appear that Saul got "caught-up" in the office, instead of the *operation* of that office, and the *anointing* attached to that office. The further Saul operated in the office, without an altar, the further his actions became more political instead of spiritual. The same Saul who was anointed by the man of God, to operate in spiritual matters, altered his motives in the process of time because of having no altars. It is a good thing and a *God* thing to protect initial motives with altars.

Now, let's take the same principle and look at King David's life. His motives created a memorial that outlived him, and because he always found a place to fall prostrate before God, even in his weakest moments, he was elevated in the office to places that he could not have ever fathomed or reached on his own—to the point that people wrote songs about him, and his memorial has come up in both the scriptures and in our lives.

The Bible states in **Acts 13:22**, *"And when he had removed him, he raised up unto them David to be their king; to whom also he gave testimony, and said, I have found David the son of Jesse, a man after mine own heart, which shall fulfil all my will."*

So, when we try the spirits, we are trying the motives—not judging the *person,* but the spirit that's attached to the function. When the human spirit rises up, there is something wrong with the motive. Spirits that are not from God—"evil spirits"—will always attempt to attach themselves to human motives, since they have no form (from the time they were cast out of heaven). They influence someone, then that person reacts with an action, which is voiced with a motive in mind.

For instance, take the action of the damsel in the book of Acts in the Bible, chapter 16. It states that this damsel said about the Apostle Paul and those with him, **Acts 16:17**, *"The same followed Paul and us, and cried, saying, These men are the servants of the most high God, which* *shew unto us the way of salvation."* Now, at face value, her statement alone appears to be valid, good, and of right motives. However, when you take the entire summation of scripture here, the context reveals another motive. Let's read a little more:

Acts 16:16, *"And it came to pass, as we went to prayer, a certain damsel possessed with a spirit of divination met us, which brought her masters much gain by soothsaying:*

(17) The same followed Paul and us, and cried, saying, These men are the servants of the most high God, which shew unto us the way of salvation.

(18) And this did she many days. But Paul, being grieved, turned and said to the spirit, I command thee in the name of Jesus Christ to come out of her. And he came out the same hour.

(19) And when her masters saw that the hope of their gains was gone, they caught Paul and Silas, and drew them into the marketplace unto the rulers,

(20) And brought them to the magistrates, saying, These men, being Jews, do exceedingly trouble our city,

(21) And teach customs, which are not lawful for us to receive, neither to observe, being Romans."

Now, we can see that their pride and arrogance was trying to get Paul, and those with him, to engage—thus attaching themselves to their vexation. This would have pulled the covering of humility off of those disciples, and would have made them vulnerable to the attacks of Satan—and there probably would not have been a Paul and Silas story, and a jailer and his family saved. It's a huge learning element here that helps us realize that our God-centered motives must be maintained at our altars, lest pride and arrogance get in the way and change those motives over time.

That's why we MUST HUMBLE OURSELVES on a constant basis, and not become a target of wrong motives—but rather, a right spirit! That's why King David asked God, in Psalm 51, after his great sin, *"Create in me a clean heart, O God; and renew a right spirit within me"* —because his motives had gone off course for a season—

but not for a lifetime. We all make mistakes, but repentance and forgiveness should come easy. That way, we don't get trapped, and, when we do make a mistake, we have no problem humbling ourselves in the sight of our brothers and sisters—and God!

On another note of "trying the spirits," we must resource God's *Logos* (the written Word of God) and the *Rhēma* (the Holy Ghost through a divine Word spoken) and make sure they line up.[1] IF NOT—THROW IT OUT! If it doesn't line up with the Holy Bible, it's not connected with The Mighty God of that Bible —Jesus Christ, the "author and finisher."

Example: I remember, many years ago, a man attempted to preach, in a pulpit, that he had a vision of three thrones with three entities on them! Immediately, the entire church resisted the vision! WHY? **Revelation 4:2,** *"And immediately I was in the spirit: and, behold, a throne was set in heaven, and one sat on the throne."* IT WAS CONTRARY TO THE WORD OF GOD! No matter who he was, his vision did not line up!

That congregation was taught not to judge—but to try the spirits. There is a difference. There are those who judge, reject, criticize, then go out to eat and talk about how wrong that person was. And then, there are those who try the spirit, reject it because it contradicts the Word of God, but then go on and pray to God for that person to come in alignment with the Word of God. Which one are you? We should take a moment here and pray that God would search our hearts and remove any condition of judging, criticism, and things that cause disunity when there is a mistake made.

So, we try the spirits based on motive and the WORD of GOD (the Holy Bible)—and in love.

Once we establish that the motive is connected to God, and aligns with His divine Word, and is ordained from heaven above, then we can move into realms and depths that have no end in faith!

CHAPTER SEVEN
EXPLORE

Exploratory dimensions of FAITH.

FAITH IS THE COMPONENT THAT REACHES INTO REALMS BEYOND HUMAN INNER-SELF DIMENSIONS. To only reach within is to deprive us of those things which are touchable and visible ("see-able") outside of ourselves—which brings us into the places where the spirit of man begins to explore the deep places of the Spirit of God.

1 Corinthians 2:9, *"But as it is written, Eye hath not seen, nor ear heard, neither have entered into the heart of man, the things which God hath prepared for them that love him.*

(10) But God hath revealed them unto us by his Spirit: for the Spirit searcheth all things, yea, the deep things of God.

(11) For what man knoweth the things of a man, save the spirit of man which is in him? even so the things of God knoweth no man, but the Spirit of God.

(12) Now we have received, not the spirit of the world, but the spirit which is of God; that we might know the things that are freely given to us of God.

(13) Which things also we speak, not in the words which man's wisdom teacheth, but which the Holy Ghost teacheth; comparing spiritual things with spiritual.

(14) But the natural man receiveth not the things of the Spirit of God: for they are foolishness unto him: neither can he know them, because they are spiritually discerned."

It's very apparent from the scripture above that, to some, these realms can appear as foolish; even the Apostle Paul says they see it as foolishness. How do you see it? The Bible clearly states that the deep things of God are spiritually discerned and are revealed—*by his Spirit*. It's not that they cannot be seen, heard or perceived by the heart. For the Word of God clearly says, *"...God hath revealed them..."*

Faith is *substance* when its ultimate goal is God, because the resource then becomes something outside of the human frame. The human frame is only capable of limited, "beginning to ending," realms.

However, faith in Jesus Christ, who is The Almighty God, leads us to "everlasting to everlasting" realms. As stated in **1 Timothy 3:16,** *"And without controversy great is the mystery of godliness: God was manifest in the flesh, justified in the Spirit, seen of angels, preached unto the Gentiles, believed on in the world, received up into glory."* GOD WAS manifest.

Establishing this as our source now gives us the basis to pursue realms without end.

How to explore is where we are headed in this chapter.

Let's talk about engaging in the realm of faith. Just faith alone comes by hearing, according to **Romans 10:17**, *"So then faith cometh by hearing, and hearing by the word of God."*

However, I want to go to another segment of faith, found in Jude, where you are building up HOLY faith. It tells us how to accomplish this:

Jude 1:20, *"But ye, beloved, building up yourselves on your most holy faith, praying in the Holy Ghost."*

First, let's come to the realization that we cannot get to realms of divine operation without divine help. Perhaps you have never allowed yourself to trust the Spirit of God to help you. But, in order to pray in the Holy Ghost, one must allow the Holy Ghost to overtake you by releasing the will.

Before you decide one way or another, let me first give you some personal stories that I have been allowed to see, while ministering across the world.

Each time the Holy Ghost took over and a person began to pray in the Holy Ghost, as Jude says, they were speaking words and sounds they did not understand.

Why is this imperative? It's the value of God taking control so He can maneuver the places that will be accessed during flight. When you engage in GOD's Spirit world, you are not talking normal, earthly, carnal, casual, knowing, or even educationally. You are speaking about entering into supernatural places that reveal God in ways that bring forth Spiritual results first, which affect our health, our body, soul, and spirit.

Not once has a person ever been made sick, evil, mad, fearful, depressed, oppressed, confused, overwhelmed in a bad way, or any other negative thing, when they allowed God to take over their spirit with His Holy Ghost—as Jude says.

Why? It's God's chosen process to take what man cannot control (the tongue—as in James 3:8) and reveal His path into Spiritual things by the Holy Ghost through us. That path causes a person to speak in a language given by God. Thus, God takes control—which is the first miracle. God is controlling what man cannot. The moment that happens, and every time it happens, you have entered another world—GOD's world.

I have heard statements after people have received God's Holy Ghost, speaking words and sounds they did not understand, saying things like:

"I have never felt happier in my life!"

"There is nothing better than this!"

"I thought I had His Spirit, but something happened to me today that has never happened before, and now I *know* I have His Spirit!"

Suffice it to say, that after seeing more than 500,000 people receive God's Holy Spirit, it has been proven over and over—this is the access to Supernatural dimensions on a consistent basis.

There are some who have come to the conclusion that the Holy Ghost is not for them. God has a word for them. Read Joel 2:28 and Acts 2:17. However, please note that this only applies to those who are flesh. If you are not flesh, you are probably not reading this book. Some suggest that "tongues" have ceased. For you, may I suggest that you ask these 500,000 people about their experience, because, if "tongues" have ceased—they cannot be speaking in "tongues."

Then there are those who are convinced that speaking in other tongues is of the devil. To those, I would ask them to go to China and ask the man who was in a meeting with us and began to speak in English for three days, each time he would pray— only to find out he had received the Holy Ghost— and did not understand *one word* of English! Here is the beautiful part. When he spoke those words and sounds, HE did not understand what he was saying, but he was not saying demonic things—he was saying things like:

"I praise you, Lord, my King, my NEW Lord!" Then he would begin to point outside the building and say, "Mountains praise Him, seas praise Him, I praise you, Jesus!"

He would touch people around him and instantly begin to pray a "loosing," as in, "I loose you, brother!"

The amazing freedom in this dimension goes on and on. I have more of these kinds of stories to solidify the facts listed above, but for now let's move on—lest it appears that I am attempting to prove an already proven point by the Word of God alone. That's not the point here. We already believe! If not, start the book over until your faith is positioned to go forward.

That being said, let's move on to the exploration stage and the "how to's" of the Spirit, once a person has engaged in "PRAYING IN THE HOLY GHOST" according to Jude.

In those realms, beyond initial evidence of His Spirit, are a multiplicity of arenas in the Spirit that bring forth so many realms of joy, peace, and righteousness. There are dimensions of health, creative acts of God, and many other dimensions that are solidified by the Word of God.

For instance, let's take a simple principle of the book of Psalms that gives us a pattern to follow.

Psalms 16:11, *"Thou wilt shew me the path of life: in thy presence is fulness of joy; at thy right hand there are pleasures for evermore."*

There are three elements here to note. The path of life, where hope starts us on a journey until we come into faith. Then, into His presence, where answers are received. It's that joy dimension where we ask God for needs to be met, and in His presence, sickness leaves, families are restored, finances are taken care of, miracles transpire! It's the place where things are taken care of based on our needs and our resolve of joy! However, let me move forward where most people stop and most church services end. Once people get what they want, they have a tendency to not pursue what He wants to do for them—not that He doesn't want to heal us, deliver us, restore us or something else similar, based on us. But, the third element here is in that same writing of Psalms—when deep moves of His Spirit are the entrance gate to greater things, and not the exit gate. It simply culminates, and there's a semi-colon, as if God paused for a moment to see if we would pursue and come closer. It says afterwards, *"at thy right hand there are pleasures for evermore."* What's so incredible is, that, previously, at the joy dimension, it's just fullness— because there will always be a cyclic rotation of needs and issues. But, when God speaks of this last dimension, He speaks of it in an everlasting form—"pleasures for evermore." From the writings, it's obvious that when God is allowed to take over—not based on our needs—He can then display His PLEASURE dimensions. I have seen how that we so often use His atmosphere for said reasons already mentioned. But then, we go from that place and go out and enjoy the normal good pleasures of life, not realizing we gave up that time getting pleasure somewhere else when it could have been the DEEP THINGS OF GOD.

Please don't misunderstand this portion of writing here. I'm not suggesting that you stop enjoying the natural things of life, but rather, consider expanding your dwelling time after He has met your need. For instance, in a given meeting in North America, we had the typical introductory of (what we, who have been around the movement of His Spirit, call) “good church.” There was singing, praise, worship, offering, etc. Then there was the preaching of God's Word, a good response, people coming to the front, crying, praying, worshipping, for a solid 30 minutes. It would have been easy to dismiss at that point and tweet, Facebook, and social media, all the great things that happened. Nothing was wrong—it's just that there was more. At that moment, something came over us, like an invitation to pursue. I suggested to the people to return to their seats and not talk to each other, but just dwell in the atmosphere. For the next hour, waves of Spiritual movements began to open up! At one point, a vision came to me. I saw, as it were, rain drops falling from an open heaven. The closer I looked, I noticed it wasn't rain—it was millions of cells falling into the building! I was overwhelmed! God said, "I am going to replenish the cells of bodies here.” I went to the pulpit and declared what I saw, and a huge WAVE of the Spirit of God hit us for the next 20 minutes! That in itself was powerful—but then miracles, signs, and wonders begin to happen! After we had finished our time with The Lord at that moment, three and a half hours had passed. That's about what it takes for pre to post football, hockey, basketball, shopping at malls, golfing (that's actually more time for 18 holes)—I think you get the point.

But, what happened next was just fabulous! I was leaving the building, and a woman walked up just flabbergasted.

She said, “Sir, it blew me away when you said it was raining cells from heaven that were going to replenish the body!”

I asked, “Why?"

She said, "Thirty seconds before, I had just asked God—because I had too many heart problems and I didn't want surgery— I said, 'God, what I really need are my cells to be replenished!'" What a divine moment it was! But here is the real probing question that should reach our hearts now, and until we pass onto our eternity: What would we have missed, dismissing at "joy?" Or, what *have* we missed because we became afraid, tired, bothered, or wanting to close-out so we could go watch, do, or take care of something that would've been taken care of—had HE entertained us in His "good pleasure."

I will close this segment with this statement. Of the 60 times "pleasure" is mentioned in the Bible, this scripture says *so much* with *so few* words. **Luke 12:32,** *"Fear not, little flock; for it is your Father's good pleasure to give you the kingdom."* The Kingdom is more than our needs being met! What else does God have for us in each of these moments that we may have walked out on, just because our time was up and we had to go put the kids to sleep, go out and eat, go to our next scheduled appointment. What if—and I will let you ponder the rest.

CHAPTER EIGHT

AWARENESS

Now that we have gone through the proving state of "trying the spirits," let's go a little further into receiving what God allows, and then dwelling in it. There is a difference between visiting a dimension and dwelling in it.

So, our "trying the spirits" is not "seeing if we like what God brings us to," but proving that it lines up with Christ.

Once our spirit bears witness, we allow our mind, body, soul, and spirit to let go.

This is where most people get hung up, because we usually have a set schedule of how long we have with these heavenly dimensions, instead of walking in the Spirit on a perpetual basis.

Whether it's devotion, pre-service prayer, or a prayer meeting, we don't really think of connecting with God's Holy Spirit as in letting Him take us wherever He desires. We have a set pattern in our cycles and not that fresh, initial approach. It's that tentative reminder of past failures and fractures that holds us back. Mistakes from the past are the worst enemy of Spiritual dimensions, because we lose the exploratory realm.

That being said, let me challenge our thinking here and probe every person who has connected with the fact of getting into His Spirit. Let me bring to our attention a few things that may similarly be on God's mind. Perhaps the greatest moves of Spiritual revivals have been on hold because we haven't explored God's world.

However, when we take a closer look at the Book of Acts, let me again bring up this passage of scripture, where we see this interaction from God's world in Acts, chapter 10.

Acts 10:9, *"On the morrow, as they went on their journey, and drew nigh unto the city, Peter went up upon the housetop to pray about the sixth hour:*

(10) And he became very hungry, and would have eaten: but while they made ready, he fell into a trance."

Let me pause here and mention that Peter fell into a trance! He had to allow himself those sensitive moments to enter into them. What would we have done? Would we have eaten, because our flesh is more accustomed to being entertained? Or, would we have fallen into a trance, because we are more aware of the movements of the Spirit of Christ. There is a drawing of God's Spirit in this 21st Century that is calling many millions to pursue and allow Him all the time He needs to carry us away in the Spirit. He wants to show us the greatest miracles yet to be discovered. Let's continue reading in verse 11.

(11) "And saw heaven opened, and a certain vessel descending unto him, as it had been a great sheet knit at the four corners, and let down to the earth:

(12) Wherein were all manner of fourfooted beasts of the earth, and wild beasts, and creeping things, and fowls of the air.

(13) And there came a voice to him, Rise, Peter; kill, and eat.

(14) But Peter said, Not so, Lord; for I have never eaten any thing that is common or unclean.

(15) And the voice spake unto him again the second time, What God hath cleansed, that call not thou common.

(16) This was done thrice: and the vessel was received up again into heaven."

By the time God released Peter back into the "normal" world, He had dealt with Peter about so many aspects of vision, change, culture, perception, faith, and trust. Question: How many Bible studies would you have to teach and preach to get someone to this point? WE WOULD NOT BE ABLE TO GET THIS DONE! Why?

Because Paul said in Corinthians, *"...the things of the Spirit of God...are spiritually discerned."*

1 Corinthians 2:14 *"But the natural man receiveth not the things of the Spirit of God: for they are foolishness unto him: neither can he know them, because they are spiritually discerned."*

We must allow God the one thing that we *say* we don't have — TIME. Perhaps our time has been seduced away by those things that TAKE IT!

What radio program, newscast, movie, podcast, social media, or favorite program, sporting event, or any other item not mentioned here, has ever given us what Peter received in a matter of minutes?

Why is it that Peter received that from the Lord? Was it just that God decided, "Oh, there's Peter. Let's use him"? I don't believe that was the case, based on what happened in **Matthew 16:13,***"When Jesus came into the coasts of Caesarea Philippi, he asked his disciples, saying, Whom do men say that I the Son of man am?*

(14) And they said, Some say that thou art John the Baptist: some, Elias; and others, Jeremias, or one of the prophets.

(15) He saith unto them, But whom say ye that I am?

(16) And Simon Peter answered and said, Thou art the Christ, the Son of the living God.

(17) And Jesus answered and said unto him, Blessed art thou, Simon Barjona: for flesh and blood hath not revealed it unto thee, but my Father which is in heaven.

(18) And I say also unto thee, That thou art Peter, and upon this rock I will build my church; and the gates of hell shall not prevail against it."

It's the one thing that the market could not steal from Peter; he was not seduced into the talk of what others said—and when the Spirit began to reveal—HE WAS AWARE! Peter gave himself to what was moving in that atmosphere! The movements that were in that atmosphere passed up eleven other disciples, because they were more familiar with their social surroundings instead of Jesus' heavenly surroundings.

AWARENESS! Living in a state of awareness becomes *huge* in a world that's consumed with agendas, opinions, issue-run talk shows—and the list goes on and on.

Awareness puts us in a special place. That place is repeated seven times in the book of Revelation, where the writer declares that Christ's desire is that every believer in almighty God (Jesus Christ) become aware to this point: "...He that hath an ear, let him hear what the Spirit saith unto the churches" (Revelation 3:22).

We have been somewhat distracted with the accomplishments of one hour of prayer and devotion, in that, we give God that slot of time and then shut off the flow the rest of the day. Where did we develop such a thought? Once again, let me probe the common thought.

Our reference for an hour is derived mostly from the encounter of Jesus in the garden of Gethsemane and the disciples. In that scenario, Jesus comes to them after he had been praying and they were sleeping. His hour had come upon him, and he wanted his disciples engaged in prayer. However, may I point out that this was not a moment of devotion, or a prayer meeting on a Saturday night. It wasn't even pre-service prayer—it was INTERCESSION! It wasn't about daily devotion or the discipline of prayer! IT WAS ABOUT BEING AWARE AND ENGAGING IN WHAT WAS AT HAND! He was about to die on a cross!

I understand devotion, prayer times, etc., as we have been taught—and as I've also taken part in. However, it has created this sense of accomplishment, where those who engage put their "time in" and then move on, into their day. One scripture among many comes to mind, where Paul says in **Ephesians 6:18** *"Praying always with all prayer and supplication in the Spirit, and watching thereunto with all perseverance and supplication for all saints;"* —AWARENESS!

In light of *awareness*, let me make a personal reference for the purpose of instruction here, in regard to the value of awareness. In *no* way do I wish to boast of anything, other than what Christ has allowed us to be a part of in these many years of this journey.

That said, let me share a moment—when what appeared to be common was, in reality, heavenly movements that were available around us—and became the difference in a divine move of God.

We were at home, just tending to domestic tasks as needed inside and outside the house. I decided to go outside and work on a project that I had been trying to finish for several weeks. I had work clothes on, with some tools—simply working in silence and enjoying the day outside, just tweaking away at the project. Suddenly, a strong presence came close—and I dropped my tools and went face towards the ground and said, "Lord, what do you want? What is it?" I began to feel God's presence so strong and the presence of a large angel that had appeared just behind me.

As I stayed there on my knees, it remained for quite some time. After about ten to fifteen minutes, noticing it wasn't leaving, I decided to probe a little more into what this could be for. I got up and walked towards the front of the house, and it followed me. I walked around several areas where we have some trees—and it followed me. I was quite curious at this point as to why God had attached an angel at my side. I went inside, and it followed me! For the next three days, it followed me everywhere I went. It was astounding that God would allow such a dimension to be connected for this amount of time. At the third day, we were scheduled to be in Orange, California, with Pastor Copple for a Sunday service. When my family and I got in the car, the angel was there as well. We entered into the service on Sunday, and when I stepped into their old building, about halfway down the aisle, the angel of the Lord detached from me! I realized it was for this church. God had allowed this angel to be connected to me for three days, and I did not know why.

One of the biggest problems with the natural mind assimilating to the Spirit dimension is—we want explanations! God's not into *explaining* His ways—He wants to *reveal* them. This took three days of submission without question. I wondered, but never questioned. My pondering was about *what* it was for, not *why*.

Within five minutes of being in that service, Pastor Tom Copple stood at the pulpit and said, "An angel just walked into this place!" Then, when I took the pulpit, I told the story of my experience the last three days. The prophetic world immediately opened up and prophecy began to flow. People fell out in the Spirit of God, onto the floor, and a deep move took place from that moment forward.

It appeared that God sent an angel to help them in the building program that was about to take place—and now, that church building is a beautiful, state-of-the-art facility, where hundreds worship God every week!

What awaits us in His world? He just needs a vessel who is constantly aware, and not distracted with things that disconnect us from God's Spirit-world.

I sincerely believe awareness is where the greatest moments exist in Jesus Christ.

CHAPTER NINE
NEW PLACES

Progress in new places.

"Such as I have ..." is what Peter said, in Acts chapter 3. I believe there was an impartation and perhaps that impartation took place in Acts 2, at Pentecost. Wherever it was, we know this—Peter and John looked at the paralyzed man and said, *"Such as I have..."*

Apparently, Peter carried inside of himself a miracle that he had received in a Spiritual moment, and was moved-on by that same Spirit to distribute what had been birthed, somewhere else.

So, learning the quickening of the Spirit of God takes time and practice. We must attempt to be aware of Spiritual NEW places in God, in order to later impart those things "freely given" to us by God.

What "normally" happens is, we go throughout our day and simply pass up moments of NEW places. Thus, we never develop new places that have been given to us to exercise. Thus, our greatest form of outreach becomes flyers and door knocking. It appears that we have left the element of being "led of the Spirit" to do *these* things—and, every now and then, we run into "new things" by accident or incident. I am positive there are many more encounters available to us, as such, but we aren't given to the sensitivity of those moments. However, instead of belaboring the point of "feeding the hungry" to bring revival, or giving away backpacks, or turkeys, etc., let us move further into being sensitive.

I am not saying that we should stop being a blessing to our communities, but I am suggesting that we not let our works be our path to reaching the "Ethiopian Eunuch!"[2] That's not what they did in Acts! They did NOT go to the less fortunate, they went where the Spirit led them. We tend to go to the less fortunate first, because it's the place of least resistance—where we won't be rejected. So, fear has gripped us. Being led of the Spirit has NO FEAR. When Jesus found the 12 disciples, they were not down in the poverty district of society. They were KEY people. Ask God for *key people,* and then become sensitive—and He will lead you there. We tend to depend more on a program to reap harvest than we do the Spirit to guide us. WHY? FEAR!

What would transpire if we had NO FEAR of failure, NO FEAR of criticism, NO FEAR of rejection from our peers, and JUST the "FEAR OF THE LORD." The functions that are required in NEW PLACES would be endless.

Just like a muscle cannot grow without exercise, we cannot grow in these new places in God without CONSTANTLY attempting to exercise what God quickens to our Spirit.

The MAIN reason Christian people (even leaders) don't operate in the quickening of the Holy Ghost, is FEAR.

It's easier for some people to *judge* through fear, instead of giving themselves to *doing*. If we are judging others, we normally don't have time to hear the voice of God—and much less implement new places in God.

Let's leave the deficient segment now and talk about when we *do* engage in NEW places. For instance—you walk into a restaurant and feel the Holy Spirit nudge you. What do you do?

If you don't ever get that nudge, you need to HIT THE ALTAR IMMEDIATELY! You are nearing the realm of hardness or insensitivity! That's dangerous ground, because carnality is next!

Back to our thought here (as we are now in that restaurant). The attendant seats you and Jesus speaks something to you. What do you do?

- Ask them to come to church? Wrong answer!
- Ask them if they would like a Bible study? Wrong answer!

- Ask them if they believe in God? It's a start!

Are you nervous yet? Why? Afraid they might reject you? Who are we obeying here?

Sorry to be so candid here—but, how are we ever going to grow if we are not challenged? Let's try it!

God did not ask you to invite them to church or give them a Bible study, in this case scenario. If He did, then, of course, you would want to do that. Whatever He quickens us to do—that is what we are to function in. NO MORE—NO LESS. Why? Because He is speaking to you about the entrance gate of what is going to lead that person closer to the Lord Jesus.

It has happened to the writer hundreds of times—if not thousands. Have I always listened? NO! Have I been wrong before? YES! Did God stop nudging me? NO!

And for those who believe you can never "miss it"—let me say this. When a preacher of the gospel "misses it" (though he may have preached a great masterpiece—but it was NOT a message from God), do we throw him or her out of our influence circle? NO, of course not. We actually "praise" that, because we are accustomed to preached messages. What would happen if we became accustomed to the *quickening* of God in and outside of the church—in preaching, in outreach, and in everyday life.

May I say that, if we practice these probings of the Spirit, it will lead us to dimensions of NEW places, NEW revivals, NEW harvests, NEW revelations—which are all built upon what we already have.

Once we walk through an open door in the Spirit, God begins to show us the rooms that exist in that NEW place. *"In my Father's house are many mansions..."*—or rooms.

Instead of mentally over-analyzing, let us feel liberty to go out in the midst of millions of needs and hear what God will have us say. Here is an example. I did walk into a restaurant, and a woman sat us down. I did feel God nudge me, and I asked the woman, "Do you believe God can speak to us?" She responded affirmatively. I then said, "The door is open before." That doesn't seem huge or life changing TO YOU or ME—but you should have seen the look of shock on this woman's face! She then said, "How did you know? How did you know? Oh my God!" She then ran off and just started crying and crying. The owner came and asked her what I had done to her. She, of course, told him nothing, but could not stop crying for a while. She served us and after an hour of being there she asked where we attend church. We did not have to invite her to church—the Spirit did the work.

On another occasion, I was working in my home (once again in work clothes) and the phone rang. A brother from another church asked if I would pray for a woman in the hospital. I asked him if he had called his pastor, since I didn't want to cross his pastor's desire, and ministry team. He said, "My pastor is out of town, and the assistant pastor said that it's not in his job description." I was shocked at that response! But, in order to not taint ministry among the saints, I said, "Give me ten minutes, and I'm on my way to the hospital." I knew that the woman (of the Catholic persuasion) was in a coma, and dying. I arrived at the hospital—but had not yet heard from the Lord on how to approach this. "*...Every thing by prayer and supplication...*" I sat in the parking lot for fifteen minutes, asking the Lord what to do.

I know how to pray. I know how to go into a hospital. But, perhaps God had another idea on His mind. It's worth asking Him, before entering that kind of environment, that's full of opinions and medical facts. After fifteen minutes, the Spirit of the Lord spoke. He said, "Go in now, and I will heal her." It doesn't always work that way—but it's worth asking before going.

I walked in, and there were about ten family members standing around her—all Catholic. I kindly asked the family, "If anyone here does not believe she will get up, please leave the room while I pray." (Jesus did that when he was about to raise Jairus' daughter from the dead.) They all just stayed and looked at me. I said, "Very well then; we are going to pray." Then I explained that, if I began to speak words and sounds they didn't understand, not to worry. That was God's Spirit inside of me, working. I had them all hold hands (to avoid the obvious signs and symbols) and we began to pray. In about 30 seconds, while the Holy Ghost was moving in that place, I felt a shift in the atmosphere—and the Lord said, "It's done!" I stopped, looked at that family and said, "It's done. She's going to be fine now!" I walked out, and in ten seconds, she opened her eyes and sat up and asked for something to eat! HALLELUJAH! Seventeen people showed up to that brother's church from that family the next Sunday, after she got out of the hospital!

(And to think the assistant pastor said it wasn't in his job description! God help those who have made this an occupation and have stopped ministering somewhere along the way.)

Let's explore and progress into these NEW places in God until we become proficient enough that it happens more and more often!

CHAPTER TEN
EXPAND

How to expand new places with help.

Now that we have established help being based on a spiritual atmosphere, let's probe into exercising, like any person who wanted to grow would accomplish through working a muscle. We don't expect that muscle to be any better by simply looking at it. That being said, let me strike the anvil and say that it's time to allow stretching—in and out of the temple.

Far gone are the days where we FEAR the operation of God! Or, are you still stuck in the proverbial fear of those days where some did not properly operate in the fear of the Lord? I pray not. We are in the 21st century—and as we proceed to the end of time, we must become more sensitive—not less. Amen? And we say, "Amen!"

If you have fear of expanding into Spiritual depths, I am positive that hell has used what God intended for growth to become a stumbling block instead of a stepping stone. I plead with those who have been affected by a "latter rain" movement, or false teaching, or "fear teaching," to allow God to lead you by His Spirit—into all Truth!

Truth was first revealed by His Spirit, prior to being revealed in the person of God. Let us then follow His Spirit, based on His Word. You cannot have His Word expressed without His Spirit projecting it.

Let's take the principle of **1 Timothy 4:1,** *"Now the Spirit speaketh expressly, that in the latter times some shall depart from the faith, giving heed to seducing spirits, and doctrines of devils;*

(2) Speaking lies in hypocrisy; having their conscience seared with a hot iron;

(3) Forbidding to marry, and commanding to abstain from meats, which God hath created to be received with thanksgiving of them which believe and know the truth.

(4) For every creature of God is good, and nothing to be refused, if it be received with thanksgiving:

(5) For it is sanctified by the word of God and prayer."

Seducing spirits are what cause theological imbalance, because the Word indicates spirits that hold the mind. It is amazing that seducing spirits can't hold my mind when I'm caught up with a vision, trance, or out-of-body experience in Jesus Christ our Lord! Those places aren't on your last social media connect, they are received when we are with Him—"online."

While in Covington, Louisiana, I was stretched beyond measure—and God taught me another principle of letting His divine instruction lead me into FIVE NEW countries to minister in. What's amazing to me is, that, each of those countries produced great meetings unlike *any* I had ever experienced before! The level of learning and reaping was astounding, and the percentage of those filled with the Holy Ghost and baptized was greater than anything I had ever experienced!

While in a prayer service that was designed as a church service—but focused on prayer—we were at the point of ministry of the Word and the engaging of corporate prayer. After about an hour, prophecy hit the place. The Lord had me prophesy to Pastor Rick Maricelli and he fell out, straight forward, on the floor—completely OUT in the Spirit. We then continued to pray. The Lord said, "Have the women let down their uncut hair, NOW!" When they did, the place exploded in worship for the next thirty minutes, and the Spirit-world went absolutely explosive!

When Pastor Maricelli awoke, he looked at me and said, "What happened here, thirty minutes ago?" I said, "Why?" He continued, "And why do all the women have their hair down?" He went on and said, "Thirty minutes ago, the ceiling and heavens opened up, and thousands of angels came flooding into this place!" It was transforming and revealing—confirming the teaching on women's hair in 1 Corinthians 11—confirmed in the Spirit-realm! But that was just for starters! It went on. He was coming down off the platform and sat down in front of the pulpit, on the carpet. I was about to head to the office, passing by him in front of the pulpit. As I was walking, the Lord said, "Lay your hand on him and pray one more time." I reached over and touched his shoulder to pray. A Spirit of laughter hit me. Then he started laughing in the Spirit. Then, we went on for FOUR HOURS!

Half of the congregation stayed just to watch and entertain what was there! It was heavenly! But in the course of those four hours, what I learned was priceless. My speaking in tongues went into dialects that I had never heard come out of my spirit chamber before, as the Spirit gave the utterance. I went through several different kinds—one of which, I am sure, was Chinese—because *that* one is kind of distinct in its sounds.

After we had come through that wonderful God-time of four hours, we headed to his home for fellowship. While we were talking, he said, "Do you remember when you broke off into those different dialects?" I responded affirmatively. He then said, "I saw your spirit going to those countries." I had never been to China at that point. Within three months, our late, great missionary, Steve Willoughby, called me and said, "The Lord just spoke to me and told me, it's time to go to China." I told him that it had been confirmed three months before, and I was ready.

There are even more details that are personal to me, that I will not tell here, but it was so supernatural and beyond anything my mind would have ever imagined. I ended up going to every country that touched that region of the world, after that encounter in the Spirit. Just for a point of Biblical reference, let me say, when God makes you laugh, He is birthing a promise—just like He did for Sarah. And also, when He causes others to laugh, He may also be applying medicine, as with a "merry heart" (Proverbs 17:22 " *A merry heart doeth good like a medicine*"). There are reasons to laugh in the Spirit, and they are not just to feel good. They have Biblical and eternal purpose in them!

Remember that there is nothing NEW under the SUN, because everything NEW is ABOVE the SUN. Let's pursue until we touch it and enter into it.

CHAPTER ELEVEN
BACK TO EARTH

Back to Earth—but not permanently.

We are not of this world.

"Back to earth" is not a coy thought of being "so heavenly minded you are no earthly good." Everyone I have ever met, who truly went to heavenly places, was able to help many people when they returned! For Peter, it was an entire family that turned into billions of people—called Gentiles! Aren't you glad he was in a trance in heavenly places? When he returned, he was able to receive what came next. It's a fact that people who walk in heavenly places *are* of earthly good! John the Revelator is still affecting people during this end time revival—and ultimately will, through the end of time—by his experience of coming "UP hither" to get what Jesus revealed. And, we thank God for those experiences which John wrote in the book of Revelation.

Though we are not *of* this world, we are *in* this world—but it doesn't say we have to stay here all the time. God's design for His 21st century church was to be in the Spirit, or, as it is written, "*...live in the Spirit...*" A lifestyle concept, which is written as such in **Galatians 5:25**, *"If we live in the Spirit, let us also walk in the Spirit"* and **1 Peter 4:6**, *"For for this cause was the gospel preached also to them that are dead, that they might be judged according to men in the flesh, but live according to God in the spirit."*

In a message recently heard while at a conference of ministers, I heard a great spiritual theologian say, "I wonder what it would be like if we lived in the Spirit and, every once in a while, we would kind of 'touch down' to pay our bills; every once in a while we would 'touch down' to take care of the necessary things of earthly life." And he continued, "But what if we could live in the Spirit and, every once in a while, just kind of descend to take care of the things of the flesh and of the world. What would it be like to pursue life in the Spirit?" At the top of my voice, I was screaming, "Yes, yes, yes!" That great man of God is a top theologian among us, leading a great Pentecostal movement at the time of this writing.

The Apostle Paul was also a great theologian, and said it this way in **2 Corinthians 12:3**, *"And I knew such a man, (whether in the body, or out of the body, I cannot tell: God knoweth;)"* Though he didn't have an explanation for it, he still wrote about it! Why? Because, it was worth mentioning for the purpose of knowing that even theologians can get into the Spirit dimension. In fact, they *should* experience it more because of their *THEO-logical* base of knowledge of this great God, who IS A SPIRIT.

The beauty of this writing is that God is saying to us, "You can, you can, you can!"

CONCLUSION

CONCLUSIONS OF THE SPIRIT REALM

There are no conclusions, because it goes from everlasting to everlasting...

In light of three things given to me while in Singapore, at 4:57 AM, while probed by the Spirit of God to not go back to sleep—let me close with this:

1) You have received by revelation and confirmed it with His Word.

It is apparent to me that things revealed by God are not to be given to opinion. The danger of opinion goes back to the discussion that Jesus had with His disciples about "leaven."[3]

He said, "...why reason ye among yourselves..." (Matthew 16:8). When God brings revelation, don't try to draw from the "bread" of the previous miracle to answer the current progress that God is bringing you into. STEP INTO IT!

Revelation aligns itself with His spoken dialogue, given to us in writing, and not "the latest miracle." To attach a revealed principle to a specific method God chose for one particular thing, is to mix principle and method. They are not the same. God uses methods for the *moment* to accomplish a particular thing. (For example: Opening the Red Sea, shutting the mouths of lions, dipping in a river seven times, etc.) HE DOES NOT WANT US MAKING MINISTRIES OUT OF METHODS! Not breathing on people, not eating bread for mouth problems, not lines of prayer, not title sermon closings, not *our* system—lest we become dependent on how we are accustomed to doing things and not allow His Sovereign Will to be done on earth as it is in Heaven.

With principle, it's settled! He doesn't change that—e.g., God saw darkness, void, and disorder, His Spirit moved, He spoke, there was light (Perhaps I will get into that in my next book). It's a principle that He put in place, and it repeats itself over and over again with different methods, depending on the situation.

Thus, with methods, it's always changing—but with principles, it's structural for spiritual things to work thereby.

2) Engage in it with proper paths.

I believe when God woke me up this morning to conclude, it was for the purpose of finishing this book on a Spiritual note. Not coincidental, but to emphatically make the point that this is a supernatural process that can't be pin-pointed in time or space from our perspective, but must be experienced and rehearsed until we "become." Or, as it is written in **Ephesians 1:9-10,***"Having made known unto us the mystery of his will, according to his good pleasure which he hath purposed in himself: That in the dispensation of the fulness of times he might gather together in one all things in Christ, both which are in heaven, and which are on earth; even in him."*

3) Exploring these dimensions is the staying power of not regressing back to where you lived before.

If we are to become familiar with a Spirit-world, which God is, then we must do the one thing that causes staying power to have its full effect in us, through us, and with us all. Explore.

Explorers like Columbus, and many others, seem to have one thing in common. Once they taste the fulfillment of landing on new territory, they don't stop! For Columbus, it was Guanahani, Bahamas, that probed the taste for more. That led him to Cuba, and onward, as his passion to explore more and more could not be quenched. A certain verbiage comes to mind, found in **Psalms 34: 8**, *"O taste and see that the LORD is good: blessed is the man that trusteth in him."*

Let me close in this manner. To *question* is to allow an open field of interaction with Satan, as was done in the garden of Eden. To *ask a question* is a very different thing. Ask the question, then move on; don't belabor the point, lest the destination is never reached. Don't worry— somewhere in that journey, the question is already answered—we just have to pursue.

When the Psalmist David continues to write in Psalms 34, he says in verse 14, *"Depart from evil, and do good; seek peace, and pursue it."*

Let us close (or continue) with this principle: When you find something in God, don't hesitate. As it is written—"PURSUE IT." It will surely lead you to *a world beyond the stars.*

NOTES

1. The Greek term logos was very popular and expressed a wide range of meanings in the ancient world. For example, Stoic philosophers believed logos was the rationale principle underlying the universe. The New Testament writers frequently used the term in different ways in a variety of contexts. Thus, in Acts 1:1 Luke referred to his first volume, a written Gospel, as a logos ("treatise" or "book"). Rhēma, on the other hand, specifically reflected a spoken utterance, saying, discourse, or speech, as in Acts 16:38 ("the officers told these words [rhēmata] unto the magistrates"). Here Brother Hernandez, using logos to refer to God's written Word and rhēma to His spoken Word, notes these two different forms of divine revelation must agree as we "try the spirits" (see 1 John 4:1–3). Ultimately, all oracles claiming to be from God must line up with the Bible or be rejected.
2. Brother Hernandez alludes to the account, narrated by Luke in Acts 8:26–40, of the conversion of the Ethiopian Eunuch, by the evangelist, Philip. This eunuch served as treasurer under the wealthy "Candace," a title for the queen of an ancient African kingdom located below Egypt. The official was reading from the prophet Isaiah while returning home from Jerusalem in his chariot when Philip encountered him in the desert. See Craig S. Keener, The IVP Bible Background Commentary: New Testament, 2d ed. (Downers Grove, IL: InterVarsity Press, 2014), 343–45.
3. Yeast and other types of leaven cause dough to rise. Jesus warned his disciples to "beware of the leaven of the

Pharisees and of the Sadducees" (Matt 16:6; Mark 8:15), two Jewish groups whose unbelief and insistence that Jesus perform signs was like yeast—or malignant cancer—that can spread undetected until it was too late. After hearing this saying, the uncomprehending disciples "reasoned among themselves" (Matt 16:7; Mark 8:16), wrongly concluding that Jesus referred to the fact they had forgotten to bring along bread. They failed to realize that Jesus was drawing attention to the insidious danger of unbelief. The disciples' faulty rationale and lack of faith had interfered with their ability to receive spiritual understanding (see Matt 16:1–12; Mark 8:1–21).

The above reference notes were provided by Dr. Jeffrey E. Brickle, Professor of Biblical Studies, Urshan Graduate School of Theology, St. Louis, MO.

SPECIAL THANKS

Since the author passed from this life during the editing process of this book, there are additional people whom we would like to thank, who helped us prepare this work for publishing.

Special thanks to Ralph Jansen, retired VP of Dun & Bradstreet Publishing Company, for his help with the final editing of this project, and for his very helpful contributions to this work.

To our subsequent editors, Rev. Adam Martinez, Tanya Martinez, Wanda Mendenhall, and Dr. June Eastridge for their assistance in reviewing this manuscript. We greatly appreciate their time in helping us present this book at its best.

Many thanks to Professor Jeff Brickle, of UGST, for his time and expertise in compiling the "Notes" section of this work. His trusted contribution is very valuable in helping readers receive clarity on particular Biblical terms and references used in this book. Thank you, Dr. Brickle, for your wonderful contribution in honor of your long-time friend, Rev. Eli Hernandez.

Thank you, Pastor Darrell Johns, for your assistance in proper Biblical notation throughout this work, and for your advice and encouragement as we finalized this writing.

To our daughter, Charity Hernandez, for her beautiful cover design, both for this book, and for the book "Maintaining Divine Operation," published earlier this year. Your Dad would have been so pleased with your beautiful work on his books. Thank you for using your talents for the Kingdom of Heaven.

Finally, we extend our sincere thanks to all those who contributed to the Advance Praise and Foreword sections at the beginning of this book. Each one of you, as dear friends of Eli Hernandez, wrote from your hearts. Thank you for your time and effort in writing such beautiful endorsements. Since the Bible states that we will "know just as also we are known"—I hope and believe that our beloved Eli Hernandez will somehow know the heartfelt words that you each wrote on his behalf. What a day that will be, when we will all be gathered together around God's throne for eternity—enjoying a *world beyond the stars.*

ABOUT THE AUTHOR

Eli Hernandez was an international evangelist. He was born on May 6th, 1960 in San Jose, California and was called into the ministry by the Spirit of God at a very young age. Though his life took many turns in his teenage and young adult years, he finally acknowledged his call into the ministry in his mid-20s.

He met his wife, Kathy, while working in the city of Boston. They married in 1984 and later moved to Houston, Texas, where they worked as Youth Ministers from 1986 until 1989. From there, the Lord called him into full-time ministry as an evangelist. For the next thirty years, Eli and Kathy Hernandez traveled across the United States and the world, preaching the Good News of the Gospel, promoting God's amazing power, and witnessing great miracles and healings, Holy Ghost in-fillings, and powerful manifestations of God's Spirit wherever they ministered.

In 2016, Eli and Kathy Hernandez, and their daughter Charity, moved to Las Vegas, Nevada, from where they continued to launch their ministry. In 2020, while traveling, Eli Hernandez contracted Covid-19. He was admitted to the VA Hospital in Las Vegas. After 45 days on the ventilator (in a medically induced coma), Brother Hernandez left this life for his eternal reward. He is greatly missed by countless numbers of people—yet his ministry continues to bless many through his writings, and through the messages that he preached (many are still available on the internet).

A documentary on his life, entitled, "Man of God" (Eli Hernandez) is available on YouTube and on the ministry website: revivalinprogress.com.

Other works by Eli Hernandez include the book, "Maintaining Divine Operation," and also a music therapy project entitled, "Healing Overtures for Physical Enhancement" (HOPE)—along with other instrumental music projects. These works can be found on Amazon, as well as on their website, revivalinprogress.com.

www.ingramcontent.com/pod-product-compliance
Ingram Content Group UK Ltd.
Pitfield, Milton Keynes, MK11 3LW, UK
UKHW021924190726
13853UKWH00002B/820